(H)

BRIAN KENNEDY

Brian Kennedy

THE LAGGANSTOWN PRINTS

BRIAN KENNEDY
– THE LAGGANSTOWN PRINTS

Published to coincide with the touring
exhibition opening at the Crawford Municipal
Art Gallery, Cork, March 1996

ISBN 0946641 730

CRAWFORD MUNICIPAL ART GALLERY
Emmet Place, Cork
021-273377 / fax 021-275680

Produced for the Crawford Gallery by
Gandon Editions, Oysterhaven, Kinsale,
Co Cork – tel 021-770830 / fax 021-770755

Design   John O'Regan
                (© Gandon, 1996)
Photography   John Searle (prints)
                Pat Looby (studio)
Production   Nicola Dearey (Gandon)
Printing   Betaprint, Dublin
Binding   Kenny's Bindery, Galway
Distribution   Gandon, Kinsale
                (and its overseas agents)

This publication was grant-aided by
An Chomhairle Ealaíon / The Arts Council
City of Cork VEC

Crawford Municipal Art Gallery, Cork
23 March – 2 May, 1996

Limerick City Gallery of Art
8 May – 25 May, 1996

Temple Bar Gallery, Dublin
31 May – 23 June 1996

Foreword

THE UNIQUE NATURE OF BRIAN KENNEDY'S MONOPRINTS OWES MUCH TO HIS SENSITIVE USE OF colour. Compressed by heavy weights, layers of ink are absorbed into the sheets of paper, creating sonorous yet emphatic bands of colour. The subtlety of his colour is particularly effective because of the stark strength of the geometric relationships between the different panels. Curiously, our experience of colour in Brian's work reminds one more of painters such as Rothko rather than any contemporary printmaker.

Over the past three years, access to the Lagganstown printing press in Co Tipperary has been generously encouraged by David Best and Maggie Roth. This has resulted in a significant enlargement in the scale of Brian's recent prints, which has in turn afforded new opportunities to develop the abstract relationships within his work. Our appreciation of the freedom of scale in these diptychs and triptychs has been much enhanced by the absence of reflective glazing for this exhibition.

The consistent quality of Brian Kennedy's work over the past ten years has made him a highly respected artist within this country. He is a member of the teaching staff of the Crawford College of Art and Design, and has also contributed to the development of the arts in Ireland in a continuous and committed way. Well known in Cork for his encouragement of younger artists, he has worked hard on the development of new workshops and studios within this city, as well as organising exhibitions of younger artists' work.

The production of this catalogue has been made possible by a generous grant from the Arts Council. Over the past few years, the Crawford has mounted several touring shows of Cork artists' work, and proper documentation is an aid to the success of such projects. This exhibition will also be seen in Limerick City Gallery of Art and at Temple Bar Gallery, Dublin.

NUALA FENTON
Exhibitions Co-ordinator, Crawford Gallery

Brian Kennedy

ALTHOUGH HE HAS WORKED ALMOST EXCLUSIVELY WITH PRINTMAKING TECHNIQUES FOR MORE than a decade, Brian Kennedy's initial training as an artist was in the area of sculpture. At the Crawford School of Art in Cork, where he enrolled at the age of nineteen, Kennedy studied under the influential teacher Ian Bibbey, and was also influenced by the work of sculptor and printmaker Sue Melling. He graduated in 1980 and then completed a post-graduate MA in printmaking at Chelsea School of Art in London. Kennedy's student years in Cork had coincided with the popularity of Conceptualist and Minimalist art, where the process of making was reckoned to be as important as the resulting work of art; but at Chelsea, the head of the department, the technically innovative printmaker Tim Mara, resisted any attempt to impose a particular house style. In spite of this, there was a definite emphasis on figuration, with two of the eleven students in Kennedy's year even presenting live performances as their post-graduate work. Kennedy was practically alone among the print students in concentrating on formal abstraction. His work at Chelsea became technically complex, combining the techniques of print-making with the considerations faced by contemporary sculptors.

Not having come from a classical printmaking background, Kennedy did not view the process as a means primarily of reproducing images, but rather as a way of presenting ideas, particularly ideas involving the passage of time. Processes were paramount as a way of developing these ideas. Typically, Kennedy would set up acid-etching cabinets and photograph the plates each day for a month, or allow steel to rust progressively and then print the rusted plate onto paper. He was concerned as much with documenting the progressive etching of acid into metal over periods of time, as with the resulting prints on paper. Most of his work at this time was based on the Golden Section, or with other conceptually inspired methods of formal abstraction. He would build up large prints from smaller pieces of metal, sometimes printing on folded paper, moving the image across, the ink being gradually drained away. Tim Mara (who now heads the printmaking department at the Royal College of Art) was encouraging, and the atmosphere at the Chelsea, with two or three visiting lecturers a week, lent itself to experimentation and innovation.

After spending two years teaching and developing his own print-making at the polytechnics in Sunderland and Newcastle-on-Tyne, Kennedy returned to Ireland in 1983, and since 1984 has taught printmaking at the Crawford School of Art. Returning to Cork, he found the popularity of Conceptualism, as at Chelsea, had been replaced by New Figuration, with Expressionist painting and sculpture very much in vogue at the Crawford. As Kennedy recounts, "In those days, you would talk about certain artists and people's eyes would glaze over. These people had become symbols of their eras, it was important to react against them. Nowadays there is no longer the need to get away from that era, no need to react. Now one can see their work again."

The grid structure, as used by Robert Ryman or Brice Marden with its Classical art connotations, is again being used by young artists, although nowadays they are more aware of its history, and employ it as a commentary in an ironic way, rather than as an end in itself. "Like a Brigid Riley, but done out in little tablets of different coloured eyeshadow."

In the early 1990s Kennedy worked mainly with colour etchings. They were more complex than his recent monoprints, and contained a number of different elements, generally grids, rectangles, door shapes and curves, which were juxtaposed on strong colour fields. It would be incorrect to describe these fields as background, because while the overlaid shapes were often overlapped, there was no suggestion of depth or three-dimensionality. The artist carefully but unobtrusively constructed his prints so as to minimise the cues which the eye naturally seeks, attempting to establish or construct depth, or three dimensions.

Resisting this impulse to present a constructed representation of the world has been one of the most important concerns in the history of modern art, and an awareness of this issue is critical to an understanding of most contemporary art. Kennedy's awareness of these pitfalls and his skill as a technician allows his prints to exist in the world as themselves, rather than as illustrations or representations of something else. Many printmakers are unconscious of this aspect of their work, perhaps because the history of printmaking through the centuries has been so closely associated with reproducing figurative images. The techniques and the marks of their own making remain clearly visible in Kennedy's prints, enabling them to exist as works of art and as objects in their own right, with confidence, assurance and a great deal of elegance. In these recent works, the mathematical or systematic basis, inspired by New York artists such as Sol LeWitt, Donald Judd and Eva Hesse, has now been relaxed. The recent prints are less structured and more intuitive, with colour playing a more important role. Kennedy relates more easily nowadays to the work of artists such as Robert Mangold.

To make this recent series of prints, Kennedy has spent a considerable amount of time working in an old schoolhouse near Cahir, Co Tipperary, which now houses a printing studio. Using large sheets of mylar as the surface onto which he applies his colours – standard printing inks – and a large printing press to offset these colours onto equally large sheets of paper, he has created an accomplished series of mono-

prints over the past two years. "I've attempted to give the work more of a mood or an atmosphere. The point of working on a larger scale and combining the prints is that the viewer can be engulfed. There is a soothing quality in the construction of the work, laying these painted stripes of colour down. It has a quietness and a meditative air about it. The images are coming out of that impulse."

The prints are generally quite large (and have become increasingly so in the past two years), with the colour saturated into the paper and bled, or extended, right to the edge of the sheet. He prefers to work not just on isolated prints, but in series. This sequencing of prints, and particularly the recent monoprints shown in the present exhibition, has become an important part of his work. In addition, his interest in formal concerns and an increasingly confident command of printing techniques has led to a steady development in his work over the past decade.

In formal terms, the very limited range of vertical and horizontal bands juxtaposed in these recent monoprints resist interpretation. Through the twentieth century, the development of abstract art has been paralleled by attempts to codify the formal elements of painting. The Russian Constructivist, Malevich, for instance, held that the horizontal line was expressive of movement, while vertical lines represented a calm transcendence, evoking the rays of the sun falling on the earth. Frank Lloyd Wright, whose architectural and aesthetic theories were influential in the development of Modernism, held on the other hand that horizontal lines represented calm, stability, with the vertical representing movement. It is evident that, as with colour, attempts to develop universal theories regarding the meaning or significance of formal values in paintings are highly subjective, and are conditioned by cultural and emotional factors as much as by appeals to the area of so-called logic or objectivity.

Nonetheless, Kennedy's monoprints demand to be read from this point of view. His recent works are characterised by the presence of two dominant axes, vertical and horizontal. These two axes are of straight bands of colour of varying widths, running from edge to edge of the paper, alternately vertical and horizontal. These recent monoprints are intended to be shown in groups of two, three or four, so, for instance, the *Panorama* series, composed of several sheets of paper placed edge to edge, appear as one long sheet of paper. These works recall the wide landscape paintings which were popular in the last century. The eye of the observer is led through a series of bands of colour, softly bled one into the other. Bands of vertical colours alternate with horizontal in a carefully balanced progression that builds up an almost stately rhythm.

There is no set pattern to the progression or to the colour relationships which are established. Each monoprint is unique and unrepeatable. The artist clearly maintains a great deal of control, carefully mixing the colours and applying them to the printing surface with great precision and exactness, but in the actual process of printing, as the inked surface is brought into contact with the paper under thousands of pounds of pressure, unpredictable factors come into play, introducing the element of chance which is also important to the work. The colour is an integral part of the paper by the end of the printing.

In some of the monoprints, as with *Panorama II* and *Panorama IV*, both from 1995, a thin horizontal line is drawn equidistant between top and bottom. This acts as a controlling centre line. Alongside are more complex series of vertical bands. If there is a very warm area it is usually balanced by a cooler area within the composition. The artist consciously builds up a dialogue between the two, playing on the contrast between the soft, blended edge and the hard, sharp edges, where the colours are held from bleeding using masking tape. "The border device. I've used this a lot. It helps make the print more static. The image is held within the boundaries of the paper. In this recent work, I've broken away from that, and prefer the colour running off the edges of the paper. This creates a sense in which it could go beyond the frame."

Although the colours are impressed so evenly into the paper that they become part of the surface, defining and saturating the picture plane, a shallow depth is sometimes suggested through two successive printings of quite different colours, one on top of the other. All of the recent monoprints are formed in this way, of two successive colour printings. "The paper sits a half inch within the plate. When laying down the paper for the second printing, the registration can be slightly incorrect.

This is an accident, but a known accident. I shifted one panel to the left and one to the right and this is what created the narrow border which runs along the top of one and along the bottom of the other. With some of these recent pieces, everything worked, but the registration was too far out. You can't make corrections or overpaint the surface. The flaw will always show through."

The artist often uses a base-coat priming of a strong colour, which filters through the overlaid second colour. When these successive printings are combined with the juxtaposition of two or more colours used in the horizontal and vertical bands, the permutations are endless. Blue or lilac contrast with warm Venetian red or cool red. Over these, the artist lays perhaps two tones of yellow to form the final colours. Combinations of complementary colours recur frequently. A stripe of yellow with purple beside, overlaid with a red and green, giving the final colour of the bands. Kennedy has deliberately curtailed the opportunities available to him to work with a broader range of colours and effects. "Up to this I would have printed three layers of colour. But now, being more confident with the colour, I'm working with only two. It makes it more subdued. It's like the Rothkos in the Tate, the ones with the deep plum colour. They are very sonorous, whereas the paintings where Rothko uses a little yellow have more of an edge to them. If you lay down a lime green, then another colour over it, you will always have that bite remaining."

The colours used by Kennedy in these monoprints are inks made for the printing trade. Printing inks are quite transparent, although white can be added to make them more opaque. They can also be thinned with turpentine to form glazes, with dark transparent colours being laid over the base colour to form extraordinary and unexpected new combinations. The resulting colours are almost always soft, not acidic, but they do have that "bite" that the artist has admired for many years in Rothko's paintings.

Some of the monoprints in this series are conceived of as pairs. With the panorama-style works, the pairs can hang side by side to make four. The use of two colours in each monoprint, with the monoprints being paired together, sets up an internal rhythm which enhances the quiet, accomplished mood of the work. But nothing

remains static. The series continues to develop. The artist is both in control of this but also allowing the medium to define its own development. "I had initially thought of doing sets of three, but that made the whole thing too long and thin. Now, with the larger, 63 x 42 inch prints, proportionately they can take a third – so the scale is facilitating longer works. The whole thing is constantly evolving. At the same time, the moves become smaller and smaller. Very often it's a question of editing out elements and leaving things to work on their own. Then I take a break, come back two days later, and dispense with half of what I made."

Kennedy's developing interest in colour has drawn him to look again at Matisse and the late works of Vuillard, artists whose work he would have passed over as a student ten years ago. Visiting America has also been important for him, seeing the work of the Abstract Expressionists such as Robert Motherwell, Cy Twombly or Agnes Martin in reality, as opposed to magazine reproductions. He bemoans the lack of a good representation of these artists' work in European collections, and also points to the excellent facilities for printmakers in the US, where technicians are an integral part of print workshops and the work produced is innovative and exciting.

Despite the current resurgence of interest in abstract painting, artists and critics today are no closer to a consensus as to the importance of such art in the world. Abstract painters who have achieved critical acclaim in recent years have done so for different reasons. Sherrie Levine and Peter Halley are praised for their ironic approach to abstraction, but Brice Marden, whose work remains close to their's in spirit, affects no such fashionable clothing for his own paintings, which remain, for the most part, solidly based in the teachings of Albers at Yale, and, hence, derive from the Bauhaus of the 1920s. Yet there is a visual excitement in these contemporary abstract artists which transcends their diverse philosophies, and it seems that the most serious of them are still driven by fundamental aesthetic condiderations, much as the Abstract Expressionists were. If one thing distinguishes these artists from their predecessors, it is the more limited claims thaey make for abstraction. This art will not change society, they say, nor unite mankind. It is unlikely to create a new utopia. Success for these artists nowadays lies in their work being genuinely appreciated by a relatively small group of people for whom it is important. If these artists discuss their work, it is often in the somewhat hermetic terms of the philosophy of aesthetics, of line, colour, form and texture, in the difficulty of moving on from one painting to the next. The realm of the spiritual, explored by Kandinsky and Albers, that opened its tragic and timeless doors wide to Rothko, Newman and Pollock, is treated nowadays with caution by these more reserved artists.

In aesthetic terms, while there has been a movement back towards the sources of the early twentieth century – particularly the sources of Modern art – the organic and spontaneous tradition of Wassily Kandinsky has been somewhat overshadowed by Piet Mondrian's grid, with layers of paint being built up carefully, or colour laid out in studied and carefully condidered sequences. But in studiously avoiding the overly ambitious and absolutist claims of the Abstract Expressionists regarding the inner necessity of art, Marden, Halley and others, who have followed a more mechanistic style of abstraction, have also denied themselves some of the essential elements which make abstract art compelling and occasionally spell-binding. Brian Kennedy achieves more of a synthesis in his work between the mechanistic and the organic, creating works that are open, that can "breath". He allows the feelings and impressions of early winter to filter through in his series of Lagganstown panoramas, a memory of autumnal evening sunlight cast horizontally across the countryside, etching colours sharply, bringing the grassy fields and brown wind-blown leaves vividly to mind even as he lays down his layers of colour steadily and methodically in prepartation for printing.

PETER MURRAY
Curator, Crawford Gallery

BRIAN KENNEDY

MT 0946 641730 8001
769.92

Panorama II
1995, monoprint, 81 x 241 cm

Panorama IV
1995, monoprint, 81 x 241 cm

Lagganstown Panorama I
1995, monoprint, 107 x 506 cm

Lagganstown Panorama IV
1995, monoprint, 107 x 241 cm

Horizon I
1995, monoprint, 160 x 122 cm

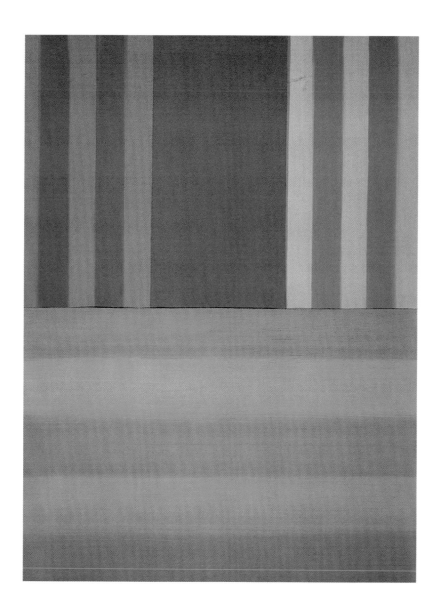

Horizon II
1995, monoprint, 160 x 122 cm

Horizon V
1995, monoprint, 160 x 122 cm

Horizon VI
1995, monoprint, 160 x 122 cm

Lagganstown Panorama II
1995, monoprint, 107 x 506 cm

Lagganstown Panorama III
1995, monoprint, 107 x 320 cm

Untitled
1995, monoprint, 107 x 160 cm

Brian Kennedy

1958 Born in Dublin
1980 Crawford College of Art and Design, Cork
    (NDFA)
1980-81 Crawford College of Art and Design, Cork
    (post-graduate course)
1982 Chelsea School of Art, London (MFA)
1982-83 Sunderland Polytechnic (fellowship)
1985- Lecturer in printmaking, Crawford College
    of Art and Design, Cork
1994 Curated *Dispatches – Print Exhibition* at
    the Crawford Municipal Art Gallery, Cork
    Lives and works in Cork and
    Lagganstown,
    Co Tipperary

Solo Exhibitions

1996 *The Lagganstown Prints*, Crawford
    Municipal Art Gallery, Cork; Limerick City
    Gallery of Art; Temple Bar Gallery,
    Dublin
    New Prints, Green on Red Gallery, Dublin
1992 *New Work*, Oliver Dowling Gallery,
    Dublin
    Artworks Gallery, Cork
1991 Crawford Municipal Art Gallery, Cork
1990 *New Etchings*, Oliver Dowling Gallery,
    Dublin

Selected Group Exhibitions

1996 Terezin exhibition, Temple Bar Gallery,
    Dublin, and touring
1995 Original Print Gallery, Dublin

Green on Red Gallery, Dublin
Cork Printmakers Show, Crawford
Municipal Art Gallery, Cork
Artists in Schools programme, Arts Council
touring exhibition
1994   Original Print Gallery, Dublin
Green on Red Gallery, Dublin
Berkeley Gallery, Thomastown
Cork Printmakers Show, Boole Library,
University College Cork
Irish Printmakers, Armoury Print Fair,
New York
Dispatches, Perugia
1993   *Eurothreshold*, Millstreet, Co Cork
Cork City Arts Show, Crawford Municipal
Art Gallery, Cork
XX International Print Biennale,
Ljubjlana, Slovenia
1991   *Impressions IV*, Galway
Works on Paper, Green on Red Gallery,
Dublin
1990   *Impressions III*, Galway
Claremorris Open Exhibition
1989   *Four Artists*, Triskel Arts Centre, Cork;
HQ – Crafts Council, Dublin
Impressions II, Galway
Oliver Dowling Gallery, Dublin
1988   Cork Artists Collective, Cork, Limerick
New Irish Printmakers, Butler Gallery,
Kilkenny
EV^A 88, Limerick City Gallery of Art
1987   *Ten Years On*, Crawford Municipal Art
Gallery, Cork; Limerick City Gallery of Art

1986   *Eight Irish Artists*, Oxford
1985   *Northern Impressions*, Crawford Centre of
Arts, Scotland
Cork Art Now, Crawford Municipal Art
Gallery, Cork
1984   *Northern Print*, Newcastle-on-Tyne Arts
Centre
Six Printmakers, Sunderland Arts Centre
New Works by Nine Artists, Chelsea School
of Art, London
1983   City University, London
Out of Print, South Hill Park Arts Centre,
Bracknell, and touring England
1982   Christie's Inaugural, London
Stowell's Trophy, Royal Academy, London
1981   GPA Awards for Emerging Artists, Dublin
Living Art, Dublin
EV^A 81, Limerick City Gallery of Art

Selected Bibliography

1996   *The Lagganstown Prints*, essay by Peter
Murray (Crawford Municipal Art Gallery,
Cork)
1994   *Dispatches – Print Exhibition*, selected by
Brian Kennedy (Crawford Municipal Art
Gallery, Cork)
'Recommended Artists', feature by Jane
Powers, *Irish Times*, 10 Nov
1993   *XX International Print Biennale*, intro to
Irish section by Jane Powers and Catriona
Fallon (Ljubjlana, Slovenia)

1992   'New Work', review by Desmond
MacAvock, *Irish Times*, 7 May
1991   'Up and Coming Artists', feature by Brian
Fallon, *Irish Times*, 18 Sept
1990   'New Etchings', review by Desmond
MacAvock, *Irish Times*, 9 Nov
1989   *Four Artists*, essay by Vera Ryan (Triskel
Arts Centre, Cork)
'Four Artists', review by Aidan Dunne,
Crafts Review, August

Collections – An Chomhairle Ealaíon / The Arts
Council; Aer Lingus; Aer Rianta; City University,
London; Contemporary Irish Art Society;
Crawford Municipal Art Gallery, Cork; Dept of An
Taoiseach; Dept of Foreign Affairs; Dept of Arts,
Culture and the Gaeltacht; Dublin Corporation;
Office of Public Works; University College Cork;
University College Dublin

Brian Kennedy is represented by:

Green on Red Gallery, 58 Fitzwilliam Square, Dublin
2 (tel 01-6613881 / fax 01-6621252), and

Original Print Gallery, 4 Temple Bar, Dublin 2
(tel 01-6773657 / fax 01-6773676)